creepy creatures

CONTENTS

Published by Creative Education
P.O. Box 227, Mankato, Minnesota 56002
Creative Education is an imprint of
The Creative Company
www.thecreativecompany.us

Design and production by Ellen Huber
Art direction by Rita Marshall
Printed in the United States of America

Photographs by 123rf (Adrian Hillman, Gerad
Taylor), Bigstock (Vinicius Ramalho Tupinamba),
Biosphoto (François Gilson), Dreamstime (John Bigl,
Joseph Calev, Xunbin Pan, Sydeen, Elmarie Viljoen),
freestockphotos.biz (Scott Bauer acquired from
USDA ARS), Getty Images (Bryan Mullennix, Gavin
Parsons), iStockphoto (Evgeniy Ayupov, Eric Isselée,
spxChrome, TommyIX), National Geographic Stock
(David Liittschwager), NHPA (Anthony Bannister);
Peter J. Bryant, University of California, Irvine;
Shutterstock (Oleg Znamenskiy), SuperStock (Minden
Pictures, National Geographic), Veer (Valua Vitaly)

Library of Congress Cataloging-in-Publication Data
Bodden, Valerie.
Termites / by Valerie Bodden.
p. cm. — (Creepy creatures)
Summary: A basic introduction to termites,
examining where they live, how they grow, what
they eat, and the unique traits that help to define
them, such as their ability to eat through wood.
Includes bibliographical references and index.
ISBN 978-1-60818-235-0
1. Termites—Juvenile literature. I. Title.
QL529.B63 2013
595.7'36—dc23   2011050279

CPSIA: 040913 PO1675
9 8 7 6 5 4 3 2

termites

VALERIE BODDEN

CREATIVE ✿ EDUCATION

You are in the woods. You pull
a piece of bark off a rotting log.
Inside the log, you see lots
of small, white bugs.

They are termites!

Termites are insects. They have three body parts and six legs. Termites have two **antennae** (*an-TEH-nee*). Some termites have wings.

Some kinds of termites have much longer wings than others

Most termites are white or brown. The smallest termites are smaller than your fingernail. But the biggest ones are about as long as your little toe!

A termite's long body and straight antennae make it look different from an ant

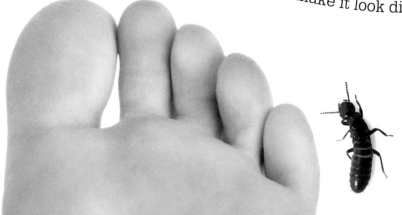

There are about 2,750 kinds of termites. Formosan **subterranean** (*sub-tuh-RAY-nee-un*) termites live around the world. They can hurt trees and buildings by eating the wood. Pacific dampwood termites are some of the biggest termites.

Pacific dampwood termites are found in states near the Pacific Ocean

Formosan termites live in warm places like Texas, Louisiana, and Florida

Termites eat their way through wood to make a nest

Termites can be found almost anywhere. But most termites live in warm places. Some termites live inside the dry wood that makes up buildings. Other termites make nests underground. Some termites build tall

mounds above the ground.
Termites have to watch
out for **predators**. Ants, birds,
frogs, and chimpanzees
all eat termites.

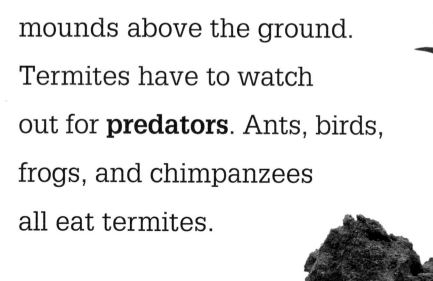

Termites begin life in an egg. Baby termites are called nymphs (*NIMFS*). Nymphs look like small adult termites. As they get bigger, they outgrow their skin. They **molt** to keep growing. Most termites live one to five years.

Termite eggs are small and white, and so are baby termites

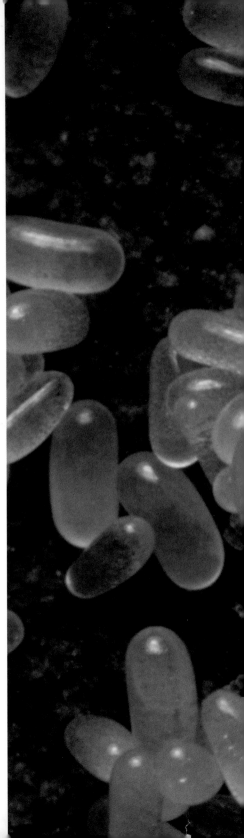

A termite's favorite food is wood.

Termites eat grass and leaves, too.

Sometimes they even eat paper,

cardboard, or cotton!

A termite's strong mouthparts can chew through many things

Termites live in big groups called colonies. Each termite in a colony has a job. The king and queen termite are the parents. Worker termites take care of the nest and collect food. Soldier termites keep the colony safe from predators. Some termites grow wings. These termites leave the nest to start new colonies.

A termite queen's abdomen (belly) can be four inches (10.2 cm) long!

Some kinds of termites harm people's houses. But in other places, people eat termites or use them as medicine. Some people travel to see huge termite mounds. It can be fun finding and watching these hungry creepy creatures!

Some termite mounds look like towers (opposite) or castles (above)

MAKE A TERMITE

You can make your own termite out of paper and cardboard. First, cut three oval (egg) shapes out of a piece of white construction paper. Glue the ovals together to make three body parts. Termites like to eat paper and wood, so glue some small pieces of brown paper, cardboard, or bark all over your termite. Cut two small strips of paper for antennae. Glue them to the top of the head. Finally, cut out six small paper rectangles, and glue three on each side of your termite for legs.

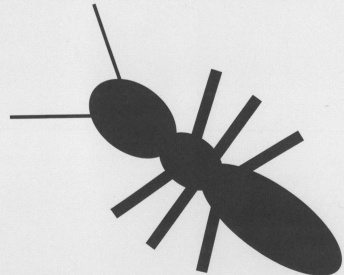

GLOSSARY

antennae: feelers on the heads of some insects that are used to touch, smell, and taste things

molt: to lose a shell or layer of skin and grow a new, larger one

predators: animals that kill and eat other animals

subterranean: under the ground

READ MORE

Claybourne, Anna. *Ants and Termites*. North Mankato, Minn.: Stargazer Books, 2004.

Rustad, Martha E. H. *Termites*. Minneapolis: Bellwether Media, 2008.

WEB SITES

National Wildlife Federation: Termite Maze Game

http://www.nwf.org/Kids/Ranger-Rick/Games/Termite-Maze-Game.aspx

Try to find your way through a termite maze and learn facts about termites.

Wood Magic Show: Kids' Section

http://woodmagic.vt.edu/kids/index.htm

Learn more about termites and their effect on trees.

INDEX

apricot oat bars

makes 10

corn oil, for oiling

6 oz/175 g polyunsaturated
spread

scant $^1/_2$ cup raw brown sugar

$^1/_8$ cup honey

scant 1 cup dried apricots,
chopped

2 tsp sesame seeds

$2^1/_2$ cups rolled oats

Preheat the oven to 350°F/180°C. Very lightly oil a $10^1/_2$- x $6^1/_2$-inch/26- x 17-cm shallow baking pan.

Put the spread, sugar, and honey into a small pan over low heat and heat until the ingredients have melted together—do not boil. When the ingredients are warm and well combined, stir in the apricots, sesame seeds, and oats.

Spoon the mixture into the prepared pan and lightly level with the back of a spoon. Cook in the preheated oven for 20–25 minutes, or until golden brown. Remove from the oven, cut into 10 squares, and let cool completely before removing from the baking pan. Store the oat bars in an airtight container and consume within 2–3 days.

Index